I'VE NEVER THOUGHT
OF IT THAT WAY

JOHN PFEIFER

dustjacket

Copyright © 2012

ISBN: 978-1-937602-10-9

Dust Jacket Press
PO Box 721243
Oklahoma City, OK 73172
www.dustjacket.com <http://www.dustjacket.com>
800-495-0192

Graphic Design: Lyn Rayn

I would like to thank my wife Glenda, my children, and ministry partners who stand beside me.

Many thanks to my friend Stan Toler who encouraged me to write this book. As well as the team at Dust Jacket who made this book possible.

CONTENTS

INTRODUCTION

It has been said, "Knowing the truth will set you free," but what is the truth?

Common sense is perception which is developed through instruction, personal experience of success and failure, and observation of other's successes and failures. To yield to things in our life without applying common sense can be a formula that allows us to be led down a path of destruction. The tragedy is that many people do not consider common sense in the equation of life. They believe that instruction is all that is needed to know the truth. Not all instruction is truth; it can be deception. We are swimming in a sea of information and misinformation bombarding us through schools, media, and the internet. Much of the information and instruction we are getting is subjective to the opinion or passion of the person or persons releasing it. There are varying opinions to most of the issues we deal with; however, you are created with the ability to develop a sense that will help you know the truth if you will receive it.

This book is designed to realign your perception by stimulating your thought. It can be used as a daily reader or for topics of discussion in group settings. However you use it, and as simplistic as it may first seem, you will need to give yourself time to fully enter into its truths. This may be your first experience in a book like this one, but after reading and thinking your way through it, you might find that it will change your life for good!

GIVING
or
RECEIVING

When holidays like Christmas come along, most of us have a wonderful experience with family and friends, but some do not. To them these times can cause loneliness and pain. This loneliness can be experienced when we are surrounded by family and friends or when we are alone. Emotional pain has been proven to attack regardless of our surroundings. To those who experience these feelings it is real and creates a time that is hard to deal with.

Many feel that Christmas has become too commercial, and they tend to complain about it because everyone is buying too many presents. This has an element of truth, but there is another way to look at it. The spirit of Christmas arouses feelings of giving and generosity in those who are open to it. We are enjoying it because of the excitement on the faces of our children and grandchildren as they open their presents. I will admit that the presents have become more numerous than they were when Glenda and I were first married, but the joy in giving was as great then as it is now. Our family has always come together and enjoyed celebrating Christmas as we give gifts to one another. We celebrate and feast! It is indeed a joyful time to look forward to.

Could it be that the power in the joy of giving and generosity is the antidote for loneliness and pain? Is it possible that this joy cannot be experienced if there are bad relationships in our life? Does the spirit of giving and generosity have the power to heal our loneliness and pain? Even if we are alone, are there ways that we can be generous and giving? Is it truly more blessed to give than to receive?

USE IT
or
LOSE IT

I was watching a commercial recently that started with a man sitting on a porch swing with his dog at his side. The voice over then said, "A body at rest tends to remain at rest, and a body in motion tends to remain in motion." It was a commercial for some type of medicine that could make you feel better, and then they read off a laundry list of side effects that could make you worse. That being said, the side effects did not lessen the truth in their statement.

A statement that I have heard that has the same meaning is, "use it or loose it", and I have experienced the reality of that statement many times. I have let a car sit too long without starting it, and when I hit the starter nothing happened because the battery had lost its charge. Everyone that owns an airplane knows that the best thing that you can do to keep it running properly is to fly it often.

Then there are the joints in our body that get stiff if we are in the same position for too long a period of time, and the muscles that are worked get bigger and stronger.

We all know these things are true about cars, airplanes, joints, and muscles, but is there a deeper truth for which these things are just a shadow? Do you know that our things and our bodies are controlled by our actions and choices? What does it take to put the things in motion that if not in motion will be lost? Could it be that we have put some things in motion that need to remain at rest? How can we know the difference?

FINDING
OUR WAY

When we travel, we use a GPS to find our way to our destination whether we are flying our plane or traveling in a car. It is a wonderful instrument that almost every traveler now uses. We just type in the address of our destination, and the GPS guides us right to the location by displaying a moving map or simply by talking to us telling of every turn that we need to make.

We have a male voice programmed in our GPS, and we call him "Jack". The female voice is sweeter to listen to, but I have been singing and traveling with two females for so many years that I just needed another guy in the car even if he is a GPS.

I have found that we will always know where we are going as we follow Jacks instructions, but sometimes we do not know where we are, and we feel like Jack is taking us in the wrong direction. When that happens, we go against his commands and almost always get off track. Jack never gets upset if we don't listen to him; he just recalculates and gives us the exact route to get us back on course.

Wouldn't it be amazing if there was something like a GPS that would guide us through life? How great would it be if there is a power that could not only guide us but recalculate our route to get us back on coarse when we make a wrong turn? Is there a way that we could find such a thing?

A GOOD DAY

This morning I got up, made my coffee, and checked the weather, which I do every day. While I was getting dressed, I planned for all of the things I felt that I needed to accomplish before the day was done. I finished getting ready for the day and my wife Glenda told me to have a good day as I left the house.

I try to make the best of my time because I am a very involved person. If you are self employed, you have to discipline yourself to do certain things because there is no one standing over you to make you do it. I feel that if I leave these tasks undone I will get behind. I have a routine of doing things at given times, and if I do not get them done, or something else pops up that demands my attention, I can start to experience some frustration. On these days, when I get home and Glenda asks me how my day went,

I find that I do not have a real sense of accomplishment. On the other hand, if everything has gone just the way I planned, I tell her it was a great day.

I am starting to realize that my good or bad days have everything to do with completing the things that I have planned to do. I can make myself a list and start checking off the items as I have completed them, and at the end of the day, if everything on the list is checked off, it seems that I have had a good day. But is this the real definition of a "good day?"

What if the things I had determined to put on my list were not really necessary? Is a good or bad day really determined by what we see accomplished? Is it possible that we are just spinning our wheels with many of these things we are giving our time to? When was the last time you re-evaluated the things that you are doing? Could there be things that we should pay less attention to and other things that we should concentrate on? How are the important things that make a good day identified?

PREPARING
for the
TOUGH TIMES

My dad was raised through the depression that our country experienced in the 1930's. He made decisions through a perspective that had been developed through tough times. Even though he moved ahead with caution, he was still always moving ahead. He did not let his lack as a boy paralyze him as an adult. Other people went through those same times and lived in a state of poverty the rest of their lives. As I reflect on my dad's decisions, I am sure that he was able to do the right thing because his life was built on a firm foundation.

There is a bible story about a man that built his house on the sand, and when the rains came, the house was washed away. While another man built his house on a foundation of rock, and when the storms came, it stood. There is also a story that I heard as a child about three little pigs that all built houses. The first little pig built a house of straw, the second built a house of sticks, and the third on built a house of stone. The big bad wolf came to the first house and huffed and puffed and blew the house down and ate the little pig. He went to the house of the second little pig and huffed and puffed and blew his house in and ate the second little pig. However, when he came to the stone house the big bad wolf huffed and puffed and could not blow the house down, so he decided to go down the fireplace chimney and eat the third little pig. The end of the story was that the third little pig had not only built a house that could not be blown down, but he had put a pot of boiling water on the fire in the fire place, and when the big bad wolf slid down the chimney, he fell right in the boiling pot and was cooked. The third little pig then ate the big bad wolf.

Do our children and grandchildren know these stories? Should we teach them that winning in the tough times has to do with diligence and proper preparation? Are they building their life on a firm foundation? Were the lessons my dad learned in the depression lessons that all of us should be aware of?

PICKING UP
APPLES

I experienced most of my childhood living in the country on a farm; however, from the time I was 3 until I was 9, we lived in town. My grandparents always lived on the farm, so during this time I frequently stayed with them. One of my most vivid memories of that time was my grandparent's apple orchard. I can remember eating those apples as soon as they turned ripe. We would go out daily and pick up the apples as they fell from the tree because they would start to decay from lying on the ground. We would save bushels of apples in wicker baskets that grandma would use to make apple sauce, cooked apples, and my favorite, apple butter. Wow was it good!

Sometimes while we were picking up the apples on the ground, I would see an apple that looked just right that had not yet fallen from the tree. When my grandparents were not looking, I would climb the tree to pick that very special apple. That apple was never any better than the apples that had fallen to the ground. As a matter of fact, it would almost always be partially green because it was not completely ripe. I could not see that it had not yet ripened looking at it from the ground. I would spend a lot of energy and do something that I should not have been doing to get to an apple that would not be nearly as sweet as those lying right at my feet.

How often have we spent time and energy going after something that is not nearly as good as it looks? How many disappointments must we experience because the things we strive to obtain turn out to be sour? Do we have to wait until others are not looking to go after them? Are the best things in life lying right there at our feet?

FIXING
the
PROBLEM

Recently I was talking to a man by the name of Bob who helps out at our airport. Bob is an older, very kind man that is a pleasure to be around. We had been discussing something that had happened earlier that I had been involved in. Bob had used our tug to move our airplane out of the hanger, so a couple other planes could be put in behind it. The tug we have is old and a different motor and transmission has been put in it. Bob had asked me if I could come out to the airport and help him move the plane, but I was going to be out of town, so I instructed him on how to start the tug. He pulled our plane out of the hanger, put the other two planes in, then pushed our plane back in its place, and successfully parked the tug.

A couple of days later I needed to take our plane and get an instrument repaired. I opened the hanger door and jumped on the tug to pull the plane out on the tarmac. I hit the starter; the tug started immediately, but it was not in park so it jumped forward hitting and damaging the hanger wall.

I have had to fix many things and have learned that too many things get messed up on their own without creating another problem. I was telling Bob how much I hated that this had happened when he said the most profound thing I have heard in a long time. He said: "If a problem can be fixed with money, it is really not a problem."

Do you think that this line of thinking might eliminate a lot of pressure and worry? Could this change our perspective on what is really important? Do we put to much thought and worry on the financial cost to us? Is money the most important thing in our life?

DUMB LUCK

Luck is a common word among people that frequent gambling facilities. It is the roll of the dice, the draw of the cards, or the spin of the wheel. Those who experience winnings are said to be lucky. I have even heard of some gamblers, who seem to win more than usual, being nick named "Lucky". These people would appear to have good luck. Then there are those that seem to have no good luck at all and seem to loose every bet they make. They attempt to win time and again, but it seems that it always turns out wrong for them. They are said to have bad luck. There was a song written that had a phrase in it which stated, "If it weren't for bad luck, I would have no luck at all." If this is true, then we have no say in the matter of winning or loosing in life. We are, in some way, held captive by the forces of luck. This way of thinking would lead us to believe, that in some way, luck has made our life choices for us, and we are dumb to the outcome. Many of us just go on living and believing that life is a matter of "Dumb Luck".

If life is truly a matter of "Dumb Luck", is it possible to have any other forces at work in our life? Can we know the statistical probability of something happening? Is living on statistical probability the same thing as living by "Dumb Luck"? Could it be possible that we have the ability to know the right or wrong thing to do? Would this knowledge of right and wrong take the "Dumb Luck" factor out of our lives?

IGNORING *the* SYMPTOMS

Many times, while I am working at my desk, I have the radio playing in the background. On one such day a radio personality was telling of his experience at the hospital while having a few tests done. He had been having some physical problems, and the doctors were trying to find out what he was suffering with. According to his story, some of the tests performed were very unpleasant and even painful at times. Even though that happened, he continued to the next test. His body was hurting for a reason and it would not get any better until one of those uncomfortable test found the problem.

Just as our body gets out of order so does our life. We have things from time to time that cause us trouble and stress, and if not attended to, can ruin our life and relationships. When our body gets sick, we do not give a second thought about getting checked out. Like the radio personality, we will do whatever it takes to get well even if we have to go through some painful times to get there.

Why do we allow our life and relationships to get totally out of order while we go quickly to the doctor if we suspect that we have a physical problem? Can you imagine what would happen if we ignored the symptoms of cancer or an unbearable pain in our chest? Could it be that we are not willing to identify those problems that might take a life style change to cure? Is the consequence of ignoring the pain in our life and relationships as deadly as ignoring cancer or chest pains?

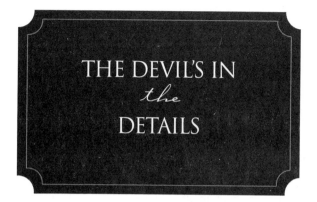

THE DEVIL'S IN
the
DETAILS

I am blessed to be an optimist, and that is why I tend to look at things from the positive side of life. Usually this is a good trait, but there are times that both the positive and negative have to be considered in making a decision. My dad used to tell me that you cannot complete an electrical circuit unless you have a positive and negative field. You can wire the positive post on your battery, but the starter will not turn over until you hook up the ground. A detail, if overlooked, which will result in absolutely nothing happening regardless of the effort put into it.

I grew up thinking that there was an angel on one of my shoulders and a devil on the other. I'm sure that I developed this mental image because I had seen cartoons depicting that very thing. The outcome of my choice was determined by which voice I listened to. The voice I listened to was a direct result of the knowledge I had of right and wrong. If I change the battery in my car, I know the right thing to do is to hook up both the positive and negative cables. I further know that the wrong thing to do is to connect the positive cable to the negative post and the negative cable to the positive post regardless of what the devil on my shoulder is saying. If I did this, I would create a dead short, and I would probably get burned badly as a result of it. My actions are a result of knowing to do the right thing.

It is not easy to admit that we miscalculated the outcome of a situation in our life. After things do not work, we have a tendency to blame the outcome on all of the circumstances that happened **after** the decision was made. Could it be that we listened to the wrong voice **before** we determined what to do or what not to do? Did we not have the knowledge necessary to make the right decision? Is the devil really in the details, or are we trying to hook up a negative cable to a positive post?

DOING IT OVER

I was raised on phrases like, "it is better to have tried and failed than to not have tried at all," and "if at first you don't succeed, try and try again." These sayings have driven me through my adult life and can encourage me when working through problems that I must deal with.

Even though these sayings drive me on, it feels better not to fail in the first place. I have had to back up and start over many times, and it is a very hard thing to stay encouraged and excited about doing it over. The excitement that comes with a new fresh idea that you believe in can suddenly go away when it did not turn out like you thought it would. Years ago, when I was building houses, there were times when we would frame in a door or window in the wrong place and have to take the wall down and tear it apart to correct it.

My employees went on making their hourly wages while we did the work over; not to mention that there was always lumber that was splintered and had to be replaced. Doing it over would cost me time and money, but it was not going to be fixed until I did something to fix it. I would then live out the sayings that I had been taught in my youth. As I reflect on these times, I know that I learned from them.

Do you think that there things that can only be learned through experiences? Is there a prevailing philosophy that is going against the time proven method of rolling up your sleeves and working your way through a problem? Is there any desire left to try and try again if at first you do not succeed? What makes a person think one way or the other?

FORGOTTEN
SPACES

Our office is located on the forth floor of a four story downtown building. The elevator is located in the back of the building and has a hall that connects to it. The hall then goes on to an emergency exit that opens into the alley. The steps are right inside the front door, so the only reason to go back to the hall would be to get to the elevator or the back alley. In trying to keep healthy, I almost always use the steps to go up to our forth floor office.

This morning I had some heavier things that needed to go to the third floor, so I used the alley door to access the elevator. I turned on the light and noticed that the hall was in need of a good sweeping. I was already a little late getting to my desk and didn't feel like I had the time to sweep it out. After making about three trips through the dirt loading the elevator, I decided that I could not put it off. I had to sweep and clean that hall before I went to my office. I knew that later in the day people would be using the elevator, and it sure wasn't something anyone else should have to walk through.

While sweeping the hall, I started to think how all that dirt had not bothered me in the least when I didn't have a reason to go there. As long as I kept using the stairs, I did not even see the condition of the hall. I wonder if there are spaces in our lives that need swept out, but we don't see them? Then, if there is an occasion that we are faced with these problem areas, do we just move on and think we will revisit them in the future? How many people might be affected by what we fail to see in ourselves? Do we need to take time to identify and sweep out some areas in our life before we move on?

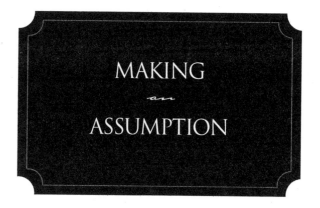

MAKING
an
ASSUMPTION

We have all made assumptions on what we think or what we are led to believe. Recently I was picking up some things at Wal-Mart, and for payment of the items I was purchasing, I slid my credit card through the credit card machine. The signature page came up and as I was about to sign it, the attendant told me my credit card had been rejected. We tried two more times and it continued to be rejected, so I paid with cash and called our office manager to ask her to look into this problem. When I got back into the office, she informed me that the credit card company said we were paid to date so we assumed that everything was alright. I sat down at my computer and started pulling off emails. I found one from a book company informing me that the same credit card had been rejected when they tried to process it. Our office manager immediately got back on the phone, and the credit card company found that, even though the bill was current, the card had been blocked due to a suspicious charge from another country. They had assumed that the only issue was the bill being current. Now there had been an assumption by both parties.

This problem came up a couple of days before we were going to be at a week long convention. A deposit for all of our motel rooms had been put on that card, and when we arrived they were going to swipe the card for the balance of the charges. If that book company had not sent the email, we would have been standing there arguing with the desk clerk that the credit card company had assured us that the card was good. That would have been a tense situation for them and us.

Do you suppose there are times we make assumptions concerning other people? Are we absolutely sure we have all of the information that is needed before we form our opinion of them? Could those assumptions keep us from building a valuable relationship? Is it possible that we assume things of the people we already have a relationship with, and it creates tension between us?

WHAT GOES IN

Being raised on a farm, we had a milk cow. We named her Dairy Queen and played with her as most would play with their dog or cat. She would lie down in the field and we would sit on her back. She didn't seem to mind at all. As a matter of fact, I think she liked the attention. Behind the pasture there was a wooded area that dad kept open to Dairy Queen and our other farm animals, so they could get shade and some relief from the flies that are always present on a farm. There were wild onions that would come up in different places in the woods, and Dairy Queen seemed to enjoy eating them. The problem was that she was our source of milk and butter, and when she ate those onions, it would ruin her milk. It would have the smell and taste of those wild onions. The milk would then have to be thrown away, and it took some time for

Dairy Queens' system to clear up from the onions she had eaten. Until we locked the gate to the woods and went in and pulled up the wild onions, the problem remained. However, once we pulled the wild onions, we could let her back in the woods so she could enjoy the cool shade on those hot summer days.

We can also eat things that will affect us. However it is not the things we eat that affect us most; it is the things that we allow in our eyes and ears that will ruin our life. It has been said that the very access to our soul is our eyes and ears. Dairy Queen did not want to ruin her milk; she just enjoyed the taste of those wild onions, but because of it she had to spend time in the hot sun until we could get rid of the problem. Do you think it might be possible that many of the problems we deal with are a result of what we have allowed in? Could it be that those things ruin our relationships and influence just like those wild onions ruined Dairy Queens' milk?

WANTING TO
DO BETTER

My Grandpa Pfeifer started singing gospel music in 1935, and my dad was a preacher, so I was raised in church. In my early years, I can remember being in church at least 3 times a week. I was a child in the 50's, and in our area, churches operated differently than they do now. The small children were expected to sit with their parents and behave themselves while the service was going on, which worked for some but not for all. I was one of those who had to be watched, so many times dad would sit me on the front seat where he could see every move I made. If I got a little too active during his message, dad would lower his hand beside the podium and snap his fingers. When that happened there would be a knot form in my belly because I knew there was going to be a price to pay. The rest of the service I would sit there not wanting it to end because of what was going to happen when it was over. I can remember that feeling of agony to this day. With all of that you would think that I would learn my lesson, but almost every week dad would have to call me down for acting up in church again. I knew what was going to happen, yet I acted up in spite of the fact that I would have to suffer for my bad behavior.

There have been times in my adult life that I would do what I knew not to do and would have to suffer the consequences for my actions. But worse than doing what we know not to do, is doing it again and again. Does the suffering for our bad choices just wear off, and we totally forget about the price we have to pay for them? Are we not capable of learning what not to do? Is there something beyond our control that drives us to do the wrong thing?

BENEATH
THE SURFACE

At one time I looked into building some townhouse apartments. I looked around for a suitable place and found a nice location that looked like it would be a desirable place for such a project. The land was level and would not take a lot of site preparation. It looked as though there would be natural drainage for the storm water, and all of the utilities were available a short distance away. It looked as though I had found the perfect spot, but upon further investigation, I found something that could not be seen.

Years earlier this property had been used as a dumping site. Because of the trash and debris, the soil would not hold a foundation. The foundation would crack and fall because the material beneath it would decay and leave a void which could not support it. When the foundation gives away, anything built on it will fall. If I was to build in such a place, all of my efforts would have been in vain.

As I look back in retrospect on my life, I can now see that there were times in my life that I built on things that would not hold the foundation of my efforts. When I did this, those things caved in and fell at my feet in ruin. I had invested and worked at it, but it had no chance of lasting because of the voids beneath the surface.

Is there anyplace that we can go to find what is beneath the surface of our lives? Are there examples we could learn from that will keep us from building our life on the wrong values? Can our efforts be blessed and not fall at our feet in ruin?

THE SURE THING

I saw a television commercial recently that was using the old saying, "A bird in the hand is worth two in the bush." I heard that time and again growing up. When I first heard it, I thought that it had a literal connotation, and I would imagine catching a bird and holding it in my hand. Later I realized that the truth in that old saying was deeper than catching a bird, and it had to do with the risk of obtaining something that you did not already have. There were, however, some contradictions to this saying in other things that I was being told.

For instance, in school I was taught that we needed to set goals and strive to do new things that would contribute to our society. The people we studied as our role models were great men of vision that wrote our constitution, past presidents, successful military leaders, and great inventors in our past, all who defied the odds of a sure thing. Even our president at that time, John Kennedy, was inspiring us to put people on the moon. That sure wasn't a bird in the hand!.

Could it be that the motive behind our actions is the real determining factor of our successes and failures? Are the truly significant accomplishments in our life things that are beyond the sure thing? Do those things benefit others as much as they do us?

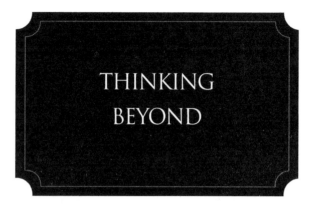

THINKING
BEYOND

We travel nationwide 2 or 3 days a week singing gospel music. Because of our local obligations, we sold our motor coach and purchased an airplane that can get us there in about 25% of the time that it took in our coach. Every week, I file a flight plan for each leg of our trip which requires me to name an airport as our destination. The internet now has web sites that can be used to accomplish this task. I type in the name of the city where we have been scheduled, and it will give me a list of airports in the area. When I first started using the program, I would choose the airport which showed the closest mileage to the city. At times, we would have to drive 40 minutes or more to get to the venue that we were to perform in. Later, I realized that the airport which showed the least miles to the city was not necessarily the best one for us to use. I learned that the mileage from the city to the airport was a given in a straight line and was not the total highway miles that it took to get to our destination. An airport close to the interstate was a much better choice even if it showed 10 or 15 miles further away. Another factor that I found I needed to consider was which side of town we were to perform on. If the closest airport listed was on the opposite side of town, it could, in reality, be further away.

When we were traveling in the motor coach, the closest mileage given was indeed the closest. I did not have to allow for straight line mileage or which side of town the venue was on to get the accurate time and distance. Some things take deeper investigation than others. Are you the type of person that will make all your decisions on the amount of monthly payment you will obligate yourself to make? Is it possible that what appears to work into our monthly budget may be like straight line mileage or the other side of town and will turn out to be a great deal more than expected? Is there a way to be able to control our life in a way that we know the real mileage of our decisions before we start a journey?

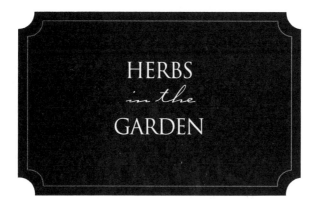

HERBS
in the
GARDEN

Acouple of years ago my son decided to have a back yard garden
and raise vegetables and herbs. The first year he found out that the
rabbits like to eat from the garden as much as he did, and he lost
a lot of his crops to the rabbits. This year, he put up a fence that
kept the rabbits out and experienced much better results for his
labor. As he was showing me all of his green beans, carrots, straw
berries, and herbs, I asked him about a plant growing next to his
rabbit fence. He told me that there was another one like it toward
the back of his garden and he supposed, by their appearance, that
they were herbs. We took a closer look, and they did have the
appearance of other herbs in his garden with a very slight difference
in the blooms that were forming. I then remembered the same
plant growing in my mulch beds at home and realized that it was

a weed that was blooming and getting ready to multiply. My son then knew to pull it out and stop it from robbing nutrients from the soil that were needed by the vegetables and herbs.

Though I do not have a lot of experience with an herb garden, I realized that it can have a lot of relevance to our everyday life.

Sometimes there are things in our life that we need to guard against like the rabbits in the garden by building a barrier between us and them. Other times there are things in our life that we mistake for peace and happiness, and all the while they are robbing us of our life sustaining substance. How do we recognize the things that we need to guard against and isolate ourselves from? Can there be a way to tell the difference between the good and the bad when they look so similar?

GOOD INTENTIONS

Growing up dad always gave us daily chores to do. One winter morning, I was throwing hay out of the hay mow to feed the cattle which was one of my daily duties. In surveying the situation, I discovered that if I threw the bale of hay hard enough, I could get it to fall into the feeder from the mow. The other option, which I had always done, was to throw the bale of hay to the ground, pick it up again, and throw it upward into the feeder. The hard throw from above seemed to be the best option. As I mentioned, it was winter, and I was dressed to keep warm complete with a heavy coat, hood, boots, and gloves. The heavy clothing hampered my motion, and the gloves made the area between the bailing twine and the bale very tight. I had not taken those two factors into consideration. As I *tried* to make the necessary spin to get momentum for the throw, my gloves stuck under the twine with my hands in them, and the bale pulled me out of the hay mow with it. I fell across a board stall and suffered greatly from the impact. That wonderful idea turned out to be the wrong thing to do. Two things happened that I had not considered. The clothes bound me up so that I could not have gotten the bale of hay to the feeder no matter how hard I tried, and the gloves made the twine so tight on my hands that wherever the bale went, I was going with it.

Did you ever do something like that, thinking it was the right thing to do and it turned out to be all wrong? Just thinking something does not make it so. There are many important things that need to be considered in our lives, and at times we do not make the right choices. How do we align out thought processes, so that we make the right decisions?

AVOIDING
the
WORSE

As the weather patterns change from early spring to summer, we experience periods of heavy rain and thunder storms. Some people have to deal with flooding and destruction through this time of the year. At the very least, if there is a weak spot in your roof, it will develop a leak. We can not change the inevitable. Storms will come, and we have no power to stop them. We do, however, have ways of dealing with the effect that they have on us.

For instance, those who live in areas that experience flooding can dig their waterways deeper and build levies to hold back the extra water from the storms. If your roof is kept in proper repair, there's a good chance that the water can not find a way through it. In preparing for the heavy rains and storms, we lessen their ability to ruin the things that we have worked to create.

There are seasons of hard times and setbacks in everyone's life. Many times, they upset us and leave us badly damaged. We can not change the fact that, just like the summer storms, they will come, and we may have little or no control over them. Do we have any power to *avoid the worse* and change the effect these things have on us? Are there areas of our lives that need to be deepened, and places that need the effort it takes to build levies, so that we can contain these hard times and setbacks? Is our life like a leaking roof because we have neglected the things that keep it in good repair and weak places have developed that are letting these things in?

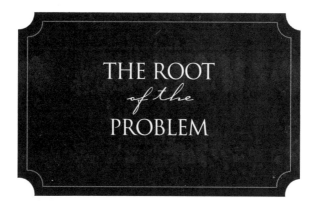

THE ROOT
of the
PROBLEM

It is good to see the grass and flowers come to life as they receive the spring rains and the warm summer sunshine. The problem is that as they flourish so do the weeds. The same rain and sunshine that give us the desirable things also give us the undesirable things that we have to deal with. I battle with the weeds in our mulch beds and lawn all through the growing season. I cut the weeds down, I spray them with weed killer, I put down plastic under our mulch, and sooner or later, they come back. Those undesirable weeds need water and sun to grow, but they do not make the rain and sunshine bad. If the rain and sun were cut off from the weeds, the lawn and flowers would also die. I have found that if I am successful at killing the root system of the weeds, I can usually enjoy a weed free environment until next year.

Is it possible that we cut off the source for the desirable things in our life trying to get rid of the undesirable things that trouble us? Could it be that relationships are the water and sunshine we need in our life, so we can flourish? Do we cut off our life source when we cut off others? Where do we go to find the root of the problem? Is the root that keeps that problem growing in others or in us?

CONNECTING
to the
POWER SOURCE

Growing up, I learned that there is a source that provides power to everything we use. For instance, to mow the lawn I had to put gasoline in the lawn mower. If I ran out of gasoline, I had to stop, go get the gas can, and pour it into the mower. The same thing was true of our tractors, hay elevator, cars, and trucks. You had to put gasoline in them before any work could be accomplished.

We had other things that worked on electricity, and the same was true of them. There was a source needed to make them work. If there was no connection to the electricity, the tool, appliance, or light would not work. I found this out while trimming my shrubs recently. I was not paying close enough attention and hit the cord with the hedge trimmer instantly cutting the extension cord, and immediately the trimmer shut down.

I also found out that there was another element necessary to complete the process. Even though I did not have the ability to make the gasoline or electricity, I had to be involved in the equation. The mower, tractor, cars, or trucks could not put gasoline in themselves. The tools or appliances could not plug themselves into the electric supply. I had to pull on the rope to start the mower, put the key in the ignition to start the tractor, and flip the switch to turn on the lights. For the power source to accomplish its purpose, I had to do something.

Are we like a machine in that we need a power source to work out our life? And even if there is such a power source, how do we get connected to it? Is there someone or something else needed to provide that connection?

FOCUS

I have a Harley Davidson motor cycle and enjoy riding it when the weather is good. I have learned that it is necessary to focus on the road ahead. A couple years back, as Glenda and I were riding through southern Ohio, a truck just ahead of us blew a recap and it flew right toward us. We were then engulfed in smoke as what was left of the tire was being ground off by the pavement. Fortunately, I was looking straight ahead and saw the huge chunk of rubber fly from the tire a split second before the smoke started. Because of that, even though we were almost immediately surrounded by smoke, I went to the center of the road and the flying recap went by without hitting us. That split second gave me time to see which way that deadly hunk of rubber was heading after it tore loose from the tire. We looked back at the tumbling recap, and it was as big as our bike.

Had I not been focused on the road ahead of us, we would have ridden straight into that recap and would have been numbered as another statistic of motor cycle fatality.

There are times in our life when it seems that disastrous circumstances and situations are flying toward us. We do not know which way to turn because our vision has been obstructed by the agony of the situation. Could it be that we would be able to avoid the inevitable failure if we keep our focus in the right place?

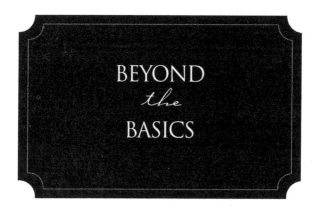

BEYOND
the
BASICS

If you watch television for any length of time you will see commercials on new products claiming to be the best. These new products range from cleaning materials to personal items. Once in awhile one of them does work better than all of the previous products available, and when that happens, you can expect to see them on your grocery store shelves or on display at the corner drug store. Those items that do not make the retail market end up either disregarded or in the "As Seen on TV" store in Pigeon Forge. It does not necessarily mean that they do not work; it just means that they were not widely accepted because the retail market could not make enough profit on them to put them into distribution.

Some of the products that do make it into the system may be popular for years, but something will eventually come along that will be better. When this happens, the previous biggest and the best becomes second place. Out with the old and in with the new! This process is a fact of life in our ever changing world that we live in. I have noticed that many of the new things coming out are for solutions to problems that we did not recognize before. We just keep working to make a better cleaner or personal item that at one time we didn't even know we needed. These things may seem good, but are we spending more just to make our life more complicated and stressful? Is it possible to get so busy trying to make life better that we forget to take care of the basic things that make it really worth living?

HIGH SPEED
EXPANSION

Recently we changed to high speed internet at our house. When I first turned it on I jumped back startled because it reacted so quickly. I did not expect such a quick response to my command. I sat there amazed as the screens would come up almost immediately with a click of the mouse. The next day I was back at my desk in the office. I turned on my computer, and it seemed to have a hard time coming up to our home page. I did not think much more about it until later when I needed to file a flight plan. I have the site for flight plans on my favorites list, and after clicking on it, I noticed my computer was having a hard time displaying the log in page. I logged in and waited for what seemed to be a long time for the flight plan page to be displayed. Then it came to me! My office computer was just doing what it had always done. In one evening I had been re-programmed to expect more. Now, what had always been acceptable was unacceptable. How quickly it had happened. Only one evening of that quick response and my expectations had been changed. I had been expanded to a new level. Suddenly, I wanted every computer that I was on to operate at high speed.

Do you suppose that our expectations can be raised in other areas of our life? Are there some people that achieve more because they have been expanded to expect more? How do we experience something above and beyond what has become normal to us? Is there something available that would work like a high speed internet for our life, expanding us all for greater things?

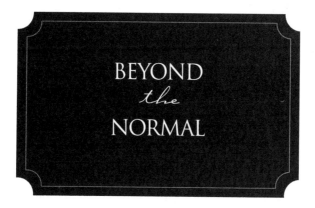

BEYOND
the
NORMAL

In making business decisions I know that it is necessary to look at all of the available information before making a commitment. Very successful companies are built on doing market analysis. There are many tools available to assist us in making proper decisions; however, nothing is absolute. Market analysis is only a study of what has happened in the past and an estimate of what might happen in the future based on human response. Even the engineering that our building codes are based on is only a fact of the past and an educated guess of what might happen in the future. The oil gushing from a ruptured pipe in the Gulf is proof of that. Bridges that have fallen are still another reminder that even our best efforts have an element of trial and error to them.

On the other hand, I have witnessed accomplishments from people who did not seem to have a chance of making them work. These accomplishments are things that a market analysis would doom to failure. Many of them do not make sense from an engineering stand point. These ideas are driven from peoples' hearts. They believe deeply in what they are trying to do, and they will not give up. Those that discovered worlds, invented marvels, and conquered the impossible were such people.

Do you suppose there could be wonderful things we are missing out on because we do not have the faith to believe? Are there some things that can only be proven by our heart? Could it be that our heart is trying to tell us of these things, but our lives are so busy that we can not hear what it is trying to say to us?

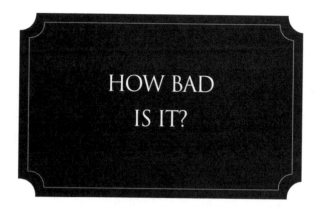

HOW BAD
IS IT?

The most frightening things I remember in my childhood were a shot from the doctor, a filling from the dentist, and a paddling from my parents. If I knew that I was scheduled for a doctor's visit, I would start to pray that he would give me pills instead of the needle. When I went to the dentist or was told that I was going to get a paddling, I knew there was no use in praying because there were no options. I would then just try to beg my way out of the inevitable. Our dentist gave you the choice of a shot to numb your tooth or just sit there and take it. Either way it was a losing situation as far as I was concerned. I usually just sat there in agony while he drilled and filled my tooth. At that point my dad would tell me, "If you sit still and don't cry, I will get you an ice cream cone on the way home." I remember the strength I would gain at the possibility of having an ice cream cone. I would be able to bear up under the pain of the drill by keeping my mind on the prize to be won. Dad did, however, overlook a few tears if I would sit relatively still in the chair.

The shot from the doctor, the filling from the dentist, and the paddling from my parents all made my life better. When I was going through these experiences, they seemed to be the end of the world for me. I could not see the benefit that was to come from going through the pain of the moment. Even though I was only aware of the fear and pain, the truth still remained. My parents knew the truth of the coming benefits to my life, so they were able to do the right thing to bring that about.

We are going to go through times of fear and pain. I realize that it is hard to see beyond the moment, but is there a possibility that it is going to make you better in the future? Wouldn't it be great to have a father that would have a reward for us that could give us hope through our troubled and painful experiences?

AN OVERFLOWING SUPPLY

I grew up on a farm where the water was supplied by a cistern. This cistern was filled as rain water ran from our roof into a large tile filled with gravel. The cistern was comprised of two chambers with a wall of concrete block separating them. The water ran down through the tile filled with gravel into the first chamber and then soaked through the block wall to the second chamber where it was pumped into our house. The water was soft and good to drink. However, unless we had a lot of rain, there wasn't enough of it. The most common way to conserve the water was by limiting our bath water, so we were cleaned up many times in the sink instead of the tub. A shower head in the bath tub or an outside faucet for watering flowers would have been unheard of because there wasn't enough water to use in such a wasteful way. Then our lives changed!

John Church, a Methodist preacher from North Carolina, came to stay with us, and he and Dad decided to put a well in our back yard. John had the ability to use a peach branch to find a water vein. Grandpa came in with his bull dozer and dug where John told him to and sure enough, after dynamiting into a rock layer, the water started to flow. Dad laid up walls, put a pipe from our pump to the well, poured a concrete lid on it, and we never ran out of water again. Mom could use all of the water she wanted to wash clothes and give all 5 children a bath in separate bath water every night. Oh how our life changed because of that supply of good water!

Does it ever seem that your life provision is coming from a cistern and there has not been any rain for a long time? Is there a way to get our provision from another source that produces an overflowing supply?

WASTED
RESOURCES

Every Spring there are stories of severe weather that make the news. This year there have been heavy rains that have caused much flooding, tornadoes that have destroyed homes and vehicles, and a broken oil line lying in the bottom of the Gulf that is threatening the economy of our southern states. Rain, wind, and oil all causing great destruction and even death; however, rain makes our crops grow, wind turns electric turbines, and oil heats our homes and runs our automobiles. The same rain that is causing flooding is giving us the food and water we would die without. The same wind that is destroying homes is giving us the electricity that make our homes more comfortable. The same oil that is threatening the economy of the southern states is powering our military and emergency vehicles that save our lives.

There are abilities and talents in every one of us that are just like the rain, wind, and oil. On one hand, they can cause us to be destructive, and on the other hand, they can make us very productive. Just like the rain, wind, and oil, our abilities and talents must be controlled and channeled. How many times have you worried about something for a longer period of time than it would have taken you to fix it? Why do children spend time and energy to take every toy out of the toy box but will not spend the same time and energy to put them back? Why do criminals master mind a crime and will not use that creative ability to improve their world? Why do some people use their influence to hurt someone when they could have used it to help them? Is there a way our abilities and talents can be controlled to make life better for us?

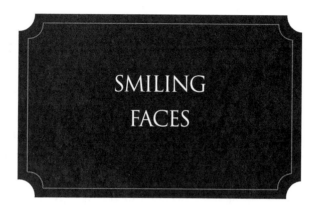

SMILING
FACES

I can remember a song that I listened to as a teenager that said, "Smiling faces tell lies." I can also remember hearing people say, "You can not trust someone that is smiling all of the time." I am sure that there are times that these phrases have held true. Some people are so deceptive that they can smile at you while all the time their motive is self serving. However, if someone is awarded a valuable prize, they will break out in smiles, laughter, and a multitude of other emotions. Did you ever notice the faces of those who are handed a new born baby? Their continence lights up as a smile breaks out across their face. You can even see that smile in their eyes. Most peoples' first reaction, when being introduced to someone that they have never met, is a smile.

On the other hand, when people have a heavy heart, their smiles are few and far between. When those people do try to smile there is no sparkle in there eyes, and it is plain to see that they are troubled. The smiles that they are able to work up are forced and are not real. It is plain to me that what is on the inside of a person can be seen on the outside of them.

We live in a real world with real troubles and there is no way to be exempt of that. You have experienced times when the smile on your face is forced, and it is not a reflection of what you are feeling on the inside. The good news is that most of us do not live our entire lives in a troubled existence. Sure we have experienced trouble, but it comes and goes and genuine smiles can be seen on our faces most of the time. Do you suppose there is a way to have a smile that reflects the good times even when we are going through bad situations? Is it possible to have a genuine smile regardless of what is happening on the outside because there is a power in us that out shines the problem?

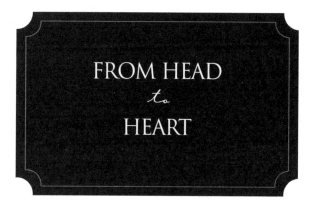

FROM HEAD
to
HEART

There are many things in our lives that we know to do and do not do them. Some of these things would make our life better, but we just do not take the necessary time and effort to work at them. We have knowledge of the right thing, but that is as far as it goes.

On the other hand, most people can remember the crush you had for the one who eventually became your mate. There was no lack of effort when it came to getting next to that special person. Nothing could stop you from being with them. You would plan your entire week around the moments you could spend together. You touched their hand and felt butterflies in your stomach, and when you would try to talk to them, you would be overwhelmed to the point that many times you would just say something silly. These feelings are usually associated with youth; however, later in life people realize that they are more than a youthful crush; they are matters of the heart. There was no obstacle that could stop you from being with that one you loved.

It has been proven that matters of the heart drive us to action. Wouldn't it be great if those things that would improve our life became a matter of our heart, so nothing could stop us from accomplishing them? Where would that process begin, in your head or in your heart?

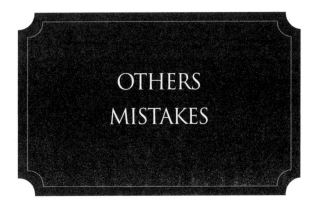

OTHERS
MISTAKES

It is so easy to see the mistakes that are made by others. Even in proof reading there are many mistakes that the author may not find, but someone else will see them almost instantly. I had an experience recently right here in our office just like that. We read over a brochure countless times looking for mistakes and saw none. Someone else read over it once and found a misspelled word.

The sad truth is that we see the mistakes others make but have a hard time seeing our own. Usually when people point out our mistakes, it offends us. Maybe you, like me, grew up hearing, "Those who live in glass houses should not through stones" or, "That sure is painting the kettle black." The problem is there are no perfect people! I have met people that thought they were, but after talking to their wife, I found they were not. There are two ways to learn. One is by experience and the other is by instruction. It is usually easier to learn by instruction, but if we get offended when someone points out our mistakes, the only thing left is the old school of hard knocks and speaking from experience that can be painful. Do you suppose we might have a deeper problem that hinders us from receiving instruction from others? Could it be that we can not get past the charter flaws of those trying to help us?

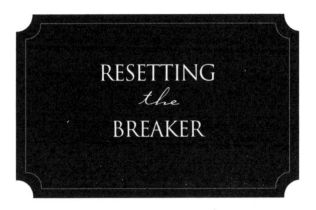

RESETTING
the
BREAKER

Every Spring, when the weather starts to warm up, we turn on our air conditioners. I can usually expect a call from one of the tenants that the air conditioner is not working. Many times they will tell me that the breaker has tripped, and when they try to reset it, it keeps tripping. This can indicate a deeper problem, but many times it is a matter of air flow and the filter needs changed. Sometimes they have not waited long enough to allow the head pressure to come down on the compressor and just turning everything off and waiting a few minutes before trying to reset the breaker will solve the problem.

In our everyday lives, we experience times when it seems our breaker has blown and our effort to restart things is not working. Many times, like the filter in an air conditioner, our lives have become so busy that the necessary breath of fresh air can not get through. My daughter Mandy said just last night that she had 6 places she needed to be through the evening, and there was not enough time to get to all of them. Just as there can be head pressure on an air conditioner compressor, there can be pressure on us and our body will shut down, and until the pressure is relieved, it will not restart. I have seen people become physically sick when the stress gets to a certain level.

It is impossible to live in this day without experiencing busy and stressful situations, but when we experience these situations, does the end result have to be a shut down? If they do result in a shut down, what does it take to reset?

GETTING UP

There were four brothers in our family, and many times when the neighbor boys would come to our house, we would wrestle with one another. I was the oldest one in the group, so most of the time I would end up sitting on top of my opponent with my knees in his biceps. If they didn't give up, I just put a little more pressure on their arms with my knees, and they would cry "uncle." That might sound a bit cruel, but it was all in fun, and no one ever really got hurt. We would engage in this activity over and over.

There were occasions, however, when there would be an older neighbor boy that would join in, and he would pin me. I would then be on my back with him on top of me burying his knees in my biceps. I liked it better when I was on top not the bottom shouting "uncle."

I have found that real life lessons are very much like the wrestling matches we experienced as young boys. When we are on top of things it feels good, but when things are on top of us, it is not so pleasant. We twist and turn and grit our teeth doing everything possible to get out from under the thing that has us down. Do you suppose that some of the things we face are like that older neighbor boy I wrestled, and all we have to do is cry "uncle" and we can get up? Could we look at life as a friendly encounter with situations and circumstances that are not always going to destroy us? Do we have to always be on top to get the most out of life? Has anyone ever lived a life where they are always on top?

HANDLING
CHANGE

I know you have noticed that things keep changing. This constant changing of things is not easy to adjust to. I have a desire to be contemporary for the day, but it takes work to keep up. About the time I feel like I have a handle on something, it changes. There are changes that are exciting and wonderful, and others that make my life difficult. For instance, the technology in finding destinations with a GPS is wonderful, but some things that work just fine keep us busy replacing them because there is a bigger and better one developed. I just had to replace the memory in Glenda's computer because her facebook and email were taking too long to load. I used to be able to take a piece of sand paper and a match book cover to file and adjust the points in my car, and it would run smoothly again. Now a light comes on, and I have to pay to get it hooked up to a computer to find the problem.

With all that said, we have to adapt to change because it is inevitable. Life as our grandparents knew it no longer exist. We are dealing with a complete new set of challenges. As our desire to have more stuff increases, the pressures that accompany those things will also increase. We have bigger houses, better automobiles, better schools, more advanced hospitals, and the list goes on and on. However, along with these things we have more depression, more broken homes, violence in our schools, and an overall attitude of discontentment. With changes, both good and bad, is there anything that goes unchanged? Is there something that we can always depend on that is right and will always be there for us? Can we successfully deal with the bad and enjoy the good?

HOPING THAT IT
WILL HAPPEN

Everyone I know hopes for the best. I personally do not know anyone who hopes that they will fail; however, there are those that do. Sometimes we give it our best effort, and it still does not work out. There are some of us that have high hopes for the end result but have no idea of how to get there. For example, one might have a great desire for a new home or car, but they have no way to accumulate the finances or even to acquire credit necessary to purchase the item.

In my life, I have found that having a vision and setting a goal are absolutely necessary to accomplish the things I hope for, but like others, everything I hoped for did not happen. When I was in high school I hoped of becoming a basketball star. I always made the team and was awarded a letter each year, but I never was the star that I dreamed of becoming. At the time, it consumed me and

I worked as hard as I could to accomplish it. Later in life, as I started into business, I realized that being a high school basketball star would not have helped me beyond my high school years. I was 5 feet 10 inches tall, and it would not have been my ultimate future. Being a basketball star would not have even made a difference in my opportunity to attend college. I was awarded a scholarship, as it was, for academics and music which was just as good as an athletic scholarship.

Could it be that many of our hopes and dreams are misguided? Do things look different after a while, and we suddenly realize these things are not as important as we first thought they were? Are there things happening that are just as good as or better than some of the things we are hoping for? Is there a way to hope for the things that truly make a difference in our lives?

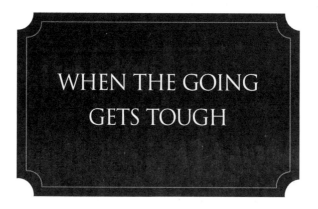

WHEN THE GOING GETS TOUGH

A saying that I have heard my whole life is, "When the going gets tough, the tough get going." I heard this most often when dad was making me do manual labor that was right at the limit of my physical strength. I remember times at the end of the day, when we were finishing a physically difficult job, that I didn't think I could go on. I would then be reminded of that saying, determination would kick in, and I was able to complete the job at hand. There were other times that it didn't matter how many times I was reminded of that saying; the job was just too much for me to complete. In those situations, my dad would come to the rescue and do whatever it took to finish the task.

Even though the years have come and gone since those days, I find that some tasks are within my ability and some are not. Many times those things that seem impossible are accomplished as I roll up my sleeves and work my way through them. I have seen situations that truly looked hopeless worked out as people will not give up. I have come to realize that the things which are truly beyond me have more to do with people than a physical task. Wouldn't it be great if dad would come to the rescue when we encounter things that are beyond our ability to handle? My dad has passed away, but could there be another father who has the power to help us?

PREEMPTIVE
MEASURES

One morning while taking a shower, the plastic center cap from the faucet handle broke and fell to the floor. I reached down and picked up the broken piece of plastic and noticed that it was not all there. The plastic was clear, and even though I had picked up the largest piece, there had to be smaller pieces on the shower floor that I could not see. My first thought was that if I could not see the other pieces, they would just wash down the drain, and I would not have to worry about them. About that time, I stepped on a small piece of sharp plastic. I could have stayed with my original plan; of allowing the problem to take care of itself and be washed away, or I could start feeling around on the shower floor and pick up all of those small sharp pieces. I thought of the consequences of leaving those sharp pieces of plastic under my feet not to mention that my wife would be getting in the shower and cutting her foot, so with the consequences considered I took the time to find all of the broken pieces and dispose of them in the trash can.

Every so often there are situations and circumstance in our lives that are broken. Many times we pay attention to the obvious problems that they create but do not see the subsequent fall out that can happen later. We give our attention only to the thing that we see at that moment and allow the smaller shattered things to go unnoticed until we are wounded by them later. Are you hoping that these things will take care of themselves? Do you think, like picking up the broken plastic on the shower floor, that we can make the right decisions and clean up the situation so we are not hurt from it later?

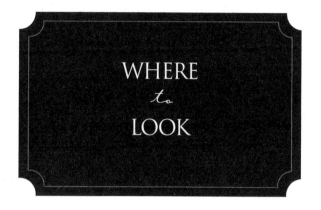

WHERE
to
LOOK

Early one winter morning, I was standing in the kitchen looking out the window, and I noticed a robin sitting in one of our holly bushes. It was only about 11 degrees and everything was covered with snow 8 to 12 inches deep. As I sipped my coffee, I could not help but wonder where that robin was going to get something to eat. Robins usually peck around in the ground to get their food, and there was no way that he could scratch through snow that deep. Yet, as I kept watching him, I realized that he looked well feed and full of energy. As a matter of fact, he seemed to really be enjoying the cold early morning. Obviously, he was getting food from somewhere that I could not see. As I continued to look out the window at the snow, I began to think of the times in my life when everything seemed to be covered up just as the snow had covered everything that morning. Going through those times, I could not see any provision in my life. I was not capable of digging through all of "the stuff" and finding what I needed.

Are we like that robin, and the provision we need is not where we are presently? Would that robin have starved to death if all he did was to sit in that holly bush and look at the snow that was too deep to scratch through? I remember reading that birds do not worry about where their food comes from because it is provided for them. Are we not much more valuable than the birds? Do we need to quit looking through the window that we have always looked through and go to where the provision is?

JOY IN REJOICING

Understanding is a wonderful thing, but there are times when I look around me and do not understand why certain things happen. From my perspective, they just don't look like the right thing, and if I had control of the issue, I would see to it that it turned out differently. Sometimes the thing looks so upside down that I have trouble getting it off my mind, and I even allow it to affect my attitude.

We have been involved in some of the Gaither Video Series tapings, and while we were doing one, Bill Gaither made a statement that incorporated a deep truth. We were talking about music awards and he said, "No one likes awards until they win one." He was right! I can remember looking at award winners over the years and wondering to myself how they had won. I have found myself looking at the national music charts and thinking that our song was better than the ones ahead of it. How about you? Have you ever had a co-worker get a raise or promotion that you feel you deserved? Have you had a friend or family member get a new car or a new home and you had to force a smile when they told you about it? It has been said that *the true measure of ones character is the ability to rejoice when your peers are elevated above you.* Are these feelings we have character flaws, personality traits, or something much deeper? Is it possible to truly rejoice when our peers are elevated above us and feel the joy they are experiencing, even though their good fortune is not ours?

COMFORT IN
KNOWING

Recently, while in Florida, we were loading in our equipment for a concert. I had a sore right ankle, and while pulling a road case up an incline, I favored it putting my back in a twist. Suddenly a sharp pain went through my lower back, and I was bent over and finding it very difficult to stand up straight. My back had twisted badly enough that I was unable to continue helping with the load in. Through the concert, the pain continued and increased while I was playing my trumpet selections.

The next day we flew home, and I had trouble walking through the airports and pulling my cases, so my wife Glenda, my sister Candy, and our other singer Mary pulled my cases and theirs. This was not something that I really liked because I felt like a wimp allowing the women to do all the work; however, I had no choice.

After we arrived home, I was able to get into a doctor that took a number of x-rays, which included motion x-rays, of my back, neck, and hips. He put me on a water massage table and then relieved some of the pressure on my spine that the twist had caused. He explained the x-rays as he showed them to me. He said that the spacing between my vertebrae was very even; that there were no spurs in any of my joints, and I had very good motion. He even said that had it not been for a fracture in my lower back, that had happened when I was a teenager, he would use my x-rays for a poster.

He had taken those x-rays before he had done anything to relieve the pain in my back, but when he explained to me that my back and joints were that of a young man, it made me feel better. For days my back was as sore as when I stepped into the doctors' office, but I was able to put it out of my mind because of the good report he had given me. Do you suppose there is a type of x-ray for our life that could show us the inner truth of what we are going through? If we could discover this would we be able to put a lot of things out of our mind that we are now hurting over?

DRY TIMES

I am writing this article while in Florida, and the sunshine is bright and warm. It brings back memories of my anticipation for summer vacation when I was in school. I looked forward to all of the fun things that summer would bring, even though dad would make me work the garden most mornings. The adventures that could be experienced in the creek that ran through our little farm were too numerous to mention. Making a baseball diamond in the pasture field and pitching our tents in the woods to sleep in at night added to the excitement and constituted hours of fun. Four hours in the garden then eight to twelve hours having the time of our lives.

Looking back on the things that occupied our time and seemed to be the best thing on the face of this earth, I realize that we were enjoying the simple things in life. Our true enjoyment came from a worry free existence. I did not one time wonder if mom would have enough food in the kitchen to fix our next meal or that dad would have enough money to pay the taxes on our little farm. We were actually contributing to our lively hood by working the garden each morning, but it never crossed my mind. I just did what was expected of me and didn't even think of the end result. I knew from experience that there was going to be a harvest from our garden and mom would prepare that food year around. There were times that we would have to haul water to the garden to make it grow, but I didn't give it a second thought. It was a dry summer, so we hauled water. It was just what happened when we had a lack of rain. It sure didn't effect my eight to twelve hours of adventure that I looked forward to.

We all go through dry times when things are not going the way we would like for them to go. The problem is that when we go through these hard times, it seems to affect every aspect of our lives. Do you suppose that there would be a way to haul water to these dry times in our lives and still enjoy the rest of our life? Is there a way to do our best and have enough trust to know that everything will turn out right?

REAL LIFE
EXPERIENCES

Years ago, I had some fundamental classes in drafting. I learned how to correctly lay out a print for various building projects and the accepted way to write numbers and letters. Later, as a contractor, I would draw some simple plans for my the various jobs. I learned quickly that everything I plotted on my prints might not be practical and could even be impossible to build. After awhile, I became better at knowing what would and what would not work. I was then able to guide my crew in a direction to make the job as profitable as it could be. There seemed to always be things that came up unexpected, but because of our experience, we could work them out.

I also was able to work with some men that had given a lifetime to their trade. Many of them had never read a print but could build about anything and build it right. They had learned lessons that had been passed down from the generations before them. These people before them had learned by real life experience.

I was taught values by my parents, grandparents, and teachers. For the most part, they had learned these values from real life experiences. As a young man, even though I was a hard worker, I had the wrong values. I had heard the "testimony" from experienced people, but I did not take it to heart. I was looking at life from the perspective of a set of blue prints that I had drawn without having the life experience to draw them correctly.

Since experience can be a hard teacher, is it possible that the "testimony" of someone who has been there is as good or even better that having the experience? Is there a source available to us that would give us the answers to all of these "real life experiences?"

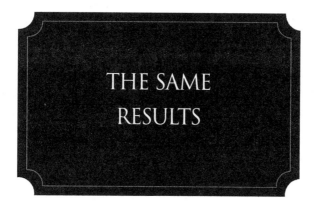

THE SAME RESULTS

My parents and grandparents taught me to never give up. Work at the task at hand until you get it accomplished. I can remember being made to keep my nose in my school books until the answer was found or the problem was solved which helped develop a good work ethic in me. I am grateful that my parents were relentless in this area. However, I have learned that there is some truth in working smarter not harder. The job we work on the longest and hardest may not be the job that accomplishes the most.

Recently we were trying to send a music track over the internet. We were not familiar with the program that we were using and could not seem to get the music saved in a file that we could send. While we were working at it, I realized that we were trying the same thing over and over and spending a lot of time doing the same thing and expecting different results. We were working diligently and long, but nothing was being accomplished. Finally, we went another route, and the music was sent a few minutes later.

One of the most important things we will ever accomplish in life is to build good relationships. The problem is that the other person has a mind of their own, and we do not always see things the same way. I have seen people struggle at trying to have a loving relationship and just can not seem to get it worked out. Could it be that the problem is not the amount of effort we are putting into it, but that we are doing the same thing over and over and expecting different results? Could it be that there is a different approach to the problem that might result in the right solution?

THE FIRST TIME

Have you ever noticed the apprehension and even anxious feelings that grip most people when they are facing the unknown? Then there are a few that seem to jump head first into just about anything you can imagine. These people that seem to have no fear are the ones that are usually very successful at the things they jump into.

The reality is that apprehension and anxious feelings are very closely related to fear. Fear of danger is a God given instinct and should be paid attention to, but this is not the fear that I am talking about. I am talking about the inability to do anything new because the fear of the unknown overwhelms you. It holds back many wonderful experiences and causes stress which will shorten our life.

After a terrorist with explosives in his underwear tried to blow up a commercial airliner, people were going to the airport hours before their flight because of the fear of not making it. They thought that the heighten security would have them waiting a very long time to get on the plane, so it would be a reasonable thing to do. However, public announcements were being made not to come so early because it was jamming up the airports and causing even further delays in processing the passengers. I am sure that very few people enjoy waiting in the airport for hours, and yet they continued to jam the airports hours early ignoring the public announcements and suffering the discomfort of standing in line holding their baggage. The fear of missing a plane actually was able to over-ride their knowledge, cloud their judgment, and stress them out.

It is easy to see how fear of missing a plane affected these people, but are we faced with circumstances in our everyday life that are leaving us as stressed as they were? Are we left standing in the long line of life holding our baggage until the load breaks us down and our life gets all jammed up? Are we really missing it, or do we just think we are?

I'LL DO IT
THIS TIME

New Year's Eve is a time of new beginnings, or in most of our lives, an attempt at new beginnings. We start out in what has been proven to be the right way to accomplish something, which is first realizing that there is a need for change in some area of our life, then admitting it to someone else, and finally DOING IT. The problem is that every step gets a little harder. We usually know what we need to change well in advance of December 31st. In most cases, we plan to make a New Year's Eve resolution for weeks or even months ahead of time. Leading up to New Year's Eve, we over indulge in the very thing that we have made up our mind to control. New Year's Eve arrives, and we proclaim to our family and friends that this is the last time for such a thing. For a period of time, we do the thing we have proclaimed to do. Then we fail and fall right back into the things that cause us a problem. Later in the year, we heal up from our failure and start planning for next year when once again we will proclaim to do better. After a given amount of failures, we just give up and live with it until it ruins our quality of life, or in some cases, life itself.

Could it be that we are missing the key? Is even our planning for a New Year's Eve resolution just a way of putting off doing the right thing and a formula for failure? Is there something that can help us move our desire to "do it this time" from our mind and emotions into our heart where changes are truly made?

JUST DO IT

When I was a child, my grandmother, who was a school teacher, bought me a book titled, "The Little Engine That Could." Many of you know the story, but for those of you that don't, it was a book written about a little train engine that had a big hill to climb. The little engine, looking at the task ahead, was not sure that he could get to the top of that steep incline. Going up the hill, he started to loose speed and momentum, and it became harder and harder until he was tempted to give up. He was repeating, "I think I can, I think I can," working harder and harder while loosing more speed and momentum. He made it half way; then three quarters of the way. About the time he had lost so much momentum that he was almost to a stand still, he got a vision of the top and changed his tune. He started to say, "I know I can, I know I can." Even though his speed was almost non-existent and his momentum all but gone, his belief that he could climb that steep hill took him over the top. My grandmother read that book over and over to me, and as a small boy it was a great time on grandmas' lap listening to her reading me a story while I looked at the pictures.

Nike coined a phrase, "Just Do It." Could it be that the troubles and trials in our life that have become mountains can be overcome by our belief and confession of victory in those situations and circumstances? Could we, "Just Do It?" Two thousand years ago there was a very special Jewish carpenter that told his friends to speak to the mountains of trouble and adversity in their lives, and they would have the ability to remove them. Do you think that will still work today? Would it be possible to not only climb over the mountains in our life, like the little train did, but to completely remove them?

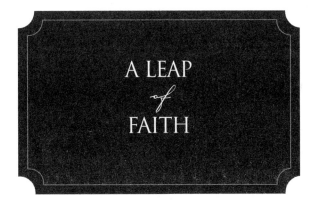

A LEAP
of
FAITH

When I was a boy, my dad took our family to a camp that was located in the mountains of West Virginia just west of the George Washington National Forest. The camp had numerous log cabins, a baseball diamond, a football field, and a river that ran through it that you could canoe on. Dad had been scheduled to be one of the speakers at a gospel event that was being held there. Camping was a wonderful experience until I decided to show some of the other boys how good I was at climbing trees. After climbing like a monkey about 20 to 30 feet up in a large sycamore tree, I proceeded to come down jumping head first from the limb I was standing on, thinking I would catch the limb below me with both hands, and swing to a lower limb close to the ground. The problem was that it was dark, and I could not see the condition of the limb I was diving for. It was rotten, and when I reached it, the limb came off in my hands, and I fell head first to the ground. Fortunately, I landed on my shoulder and not my head. I did, however, break my shoulder so badly that I had to be moved to a major hospital that had a world renowned bone surgeon to get it repaired.

There is an old saying, "Look before you leap." The only problem was it was dark, and I could not see well enough to know that the limb was rotten. Are you sure there is enough light in your life to see clearly the thing that you are about to grab hold of? What is the condition of the things you are planning to putting your trust in? What if that person, situation, or circumstance lets you down?

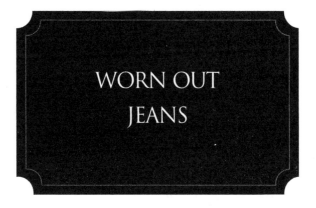

WORN OUT JEANS

When I was a boy in grade school, one of the most exciting things in my life was going to town to get school clothes. Typically, Dad and Mom would get me 2 pairs of jeans and 3 or 4 shirts that had to last me until it was time to buy school clothes again the next year. Because I was still growing, they would buy the next biggest size so that I would not completely outgrow them before next year rolled around. When school started, they were bigger than I needed; about half way through the school year, they were a good fit, and by the time summer vacation arrived, they were too small. Mom would then assign one pair to be my play jeans for cooler days and the other pair she would cut off for shorts that I would wear through out the summer until the exciting time came, once again, to buy school clothes.

As I look back on these experiences, I see that the size of the jeans never really changed. They were the same size at the start of the school year as they were at the end, and yet they only correctly fitted me at a certain point and time. The rest of the time, even though I still wore them, they did not fit. The reason for them not fitting was that I was changing and the jeans were not.

As we journey through life, things change. We change, people around us change, our situations and circumstances change; could it be that our perception of life is like wearing a pair of worn out jeans that no longer fit? Is it possible that the things that were a good fit in a certain season of our life don't fit any longer? In your life, are you still expecting yesterdays' size to be right for today? Is it time for a new pair of jeans?

ANOTHER WAY

When I travel to Indianapolis, Indiana, I have always left Washington Court House on US 35, taken it to Dayton, gone north on I-75, and then I-70 west to my destination. Like most others that travel, we now use a GPS which is a real help in finding locations that we are not familiar with. The first time I used it going to Indianapolis, it wanted me to take I-71 south toward Cincinnati. I knew the thing was not operating properly because the route to Indianapolis was going through Dayton, not Cincinnati. So, for the past couple of years when I want to go to Indianapolis, I turn the voice prompt off until I get out of town, then it will reset and take me through Dayton.

The other day our sound engineer Zach, who also has a GPS in the van that hauls our equipment, did what the GPS wanted him to do and took I-71 south to the outer belt in Cincinnati then up I-74 to Indianapolis. To my surprise, he told me that he actually saved some time going that way.

Do you suppose we are doing many things the same way because it is the way we have always done them? Could there be better routes on the pathway of life that we should consider? Is there a GPS for our life that would guide us on those paths?

THE RELAY
EFFECT

As a child growing up in the 50's, we did not have video games to keep us occupied when we were not in school. I heard 1,000 times that idle hands are the devil's workshop, so I was kept very busy. Since we did not have all of the things kids today have, we would be given jobs to do, or we would invent something that would amuse us. One such invented game, when we had all of the neighborhood kids over, was to tell a story in someone's ear, and they would pass it on to someone else and so on. When the last person had the story whispered in their ear, they would tell the story as they remembered it being told them just a moment before. The amazing thing was that the story never ended as it started. Sometimes, it was so far off that it did not even resemble the story that was whispered in the first person's ear. I am sure that many of you are relating to this childhood game.

I have found that a story related over and over never does remain the same. Many times, people get bad information or are damaged because of it. Did we learn anything from that childhood game? Can second, third, or fourth party stories ever be accurate? Are there many things that do not need to be passed on? Is there guidance available to us to keep this from happening?

A REASON WHY

Afew years ago on a beautiful Spring day, I was down on my parents' farm in southern Ohio. Dad had taken one of his quarter horses out of the barn for a little exercise. She had been in the barn most of the winter and was rather lively as he rode her up to the back yard. She was chomping at the bit as dad held her back. I was raised with horses and at one time in my life had made some extra money breaking them. Dad asked me if I wanted to take her out for a ride but cautioned me that she was full of life. I was not thinking that it had been some time since I had ridden, so I informed dad that I could very easily handle her. I grabbed the reins, threw myself up in the saddle, and dug my heals in her flank. We took off like a rocket across the field next to the house. I was riding like the wind in total control when the unexpected happened. That horse planted both of her front feet turning sharply to the left and kicked her hind feet in the air. I was thrown out of that saddle so fast that the ring I was wearing on my right hand was ripped off never to be seen again. The horse ran back to the barn, and I came limping out of the field.

This experience resulted in the loss of a valuable ring, sore mussles and joints for a great while, and the embarrassment of the whole ordeal as my family witnessed me flying through the air. In retrospect, I know that the horse should have been held back until she was worn down a bit, and that I should not have bragged about how great of a horseman I was.

There are many times in our life that situations come up unexpected. Most of the time these things set us back to some degree. The *reason for the setback* is the unexpected situation. Are we caught up in the set back or are we working on *the reason* for it? Can it happen again because the reason is never addressed?

THINKING
the
WORSE

Recently, I had something go wrong with the shifting column in my truck. I had a mechanic look at it, and we discussed trying to find a complete steering column at a junk yard to save the money it would take to purchase a new one. That evening I had some passing thoughts about needing a new truck if this one was going to start giving me trouble. I thought I might get the mechanic to start looking for a steering column. If he found one, I could get it put in, fix a few other things, and maybe sell my truck and get another one. The next day I went to start my truck and couldn't get it started. I had to put excessive upward force on the shifter until I could get the starter to engage, so I decided to drive straight to the repair facility while I had it running. I caught a ride home and got a car to drive not knowing how long it would take to find the necessary parts to repair my truck. I had been at my office for only an hour or so when the phone rang, and it was the mechanic telling me my truck was ready. I almost feel out of my chair. How could it be fixed so fast? I found out the steering column was fine, and the only problem was that two bolts had worked loose. How fortunate can one be?

After that phone call, I sat in my office wondering how many times in my life I had expected the worse and it never happened. How many times have you thought that the worse was inevitable, and it never came to pass? It is said that 80% of the things we worry about never happen, so why is our first thought usually the worse case scenario? Could we change our thought process to think of the best instead of the worse? How many relationships have we failed to build because we only saw the worse in someone? What if we were 80% wrong about that person? (Oh, by the way, I think I will keep this truck for now.)

TURNING LOOSE

Years ago, when I started in business, I felt that my success would be measured by the amount of money I would make in my life. When I had some money, life seemed better. My friends looked up to me and wanted to do me favors because to some I appeared successful. I measured everything by the amount of money that was involved in it. My decisions in life were all about money. The problem was that nothing seemed to turn out as good as I imagined it would. I would work harder and harder, make more and more, and seem to only have enough to get by. Real success, as I saw it, seemed to always be just out of my reach.

In the early 1980's, tough financial times hit, and there was not much money to be made. I was still in business, but through these hard times and a change of heart, my attitude toward money changed. It no longer absorbed me. I had started to have a greater appreciation for my family and my relationships. I sold my business at auction and never looked back.

Could it be that my love for money really hindered me from keeping it? Could my motives have been so far off that I was missing life's greatest treasures? Do you have to turn loose of things to get them in their proper place?

SUDDEN CHANGE

Recently, while landing at an airport in another state, we encountered strong gusting winds. The air traffic control had given us the speed of the wind and the gusts; however, as we were about to touch down a gust stronger than we expected picked us up and blew us sideways until we were almost over the taxiway instead of the runway. After getting lined up over the runway again, we started to touch down and another gust picked us up, and once again we were almost over the taxiway. We applied power, lined up again, and this time touched down with a smooth landing. I made a call to a flight instructor and asked him if there were any tried and proven ways to deal with these gusts of wind that were stronger than expected. He gave me a formula for increasing landing speed that was calculated using the wind and gust factor that would make it possible to remain above the runway for touch down.

We are experiencing strong winds and unexpected gusts in our country and personal lives at this time. Many people are tossed by the winds that they do not see coming. Do you suppose there is a way to be prepared for these winds? Is there a formula that would help us through and keep us on course?

BUILDING BLOCKS

If you were a child in the 50's as I was, you probably had a set of building blocks. The blocks we had were all the same shape and size with numbers and letters on them. You could stack them up to spell words or put them in numerical order. They were a perfect square and had some groves in them to make them stay in line as you stacked them.

People working together in a community are very much like those building blocks. We can be placed in order so that we make sense; however, we are not all alike. We are not all perfect squares with groves to make us stack up straight. We are very different in our talents and abilities. In relation to the building blocks, some of us might be square, but others might be round. There are others that might be triangles or rectangles. If you try to stack a triangle in with the square blocks it seems impossible. Or is it?

When I was involved in construction, I faced a fire place with flagstone. When the stones were delivered they were all shapes and sizes. We would work to find stones that could be mortared together to make a straight front. Sometimes we would have to break the stones to make them work, but the mortar would fill in the differences in the various shaped stones. Could it be that even though we are all different, there is mortar, so to speak, that can makes us all fit together? Is it possible to find out what that mortar is and apply it to our lives to fill in the differences? Could the hard times we experience just be a breaking that we need to be able to fill our position in life?

PULLING WEEDS

There is a weed in our area called water crest, and most farmers have at one time or the other had to deal with it. In a few years, if left unattended, it will take over a pasture field. It has a bright and full yellow bloom, and it can look very pretty as it totally absorbs the field in a sea of yellow. At a distance, it can look like the beautiful fields in Western Canada filled with the yellow blooms of the canola plant. Even though they can look the same, one plant is good for nothing, and the other very useful.

When I was a boy, we had a pasture that the water crest had taken over. My dad informed us that when it was in full bloom we were going to get everyone in the field and pull it all up by hand. He knew that it would be very easy to identify by its bright yellow bloom, and that when the blooms were off, it would go to seed, and there would be even more water crest to deal with the next year. We lined up across that pasture field and within a few days we had pulled the water crest, loaded it in a wagon, and dumped it in the woods where it could no longer choke out the pasture.

From time to time weeds will grow in our lives. When this happens it seems that there is multiplied turmoil and trouble coming at us. They can be deceptive and even have the appearance of something good, but they are blooming and about to go to seed which will cause even more problems. Is there a way to identify the weeds in our life? Would it be possible to pull up those things and get rid of them like we did the water crest? Would the job of pulling those weeds be easier if we had the help and assistance of others?

JUMPING OUT

I know you have heard that if you put a frog in cool water and then bring it to a boil, the frog will stay in the water and boil to death. The gradual rise in the water temperature does not affect him until it is too late because his body temperature rises with the water temperature and everything seems normal to him. All he would have to do to save his life is to make a move and jump to safety.

There is also a story of an experiment that was carried out with fleas that were captured and put in a coffee can with a lid on it. The fleas sounded like pop corn hitting the lid for some time, then a few at a time quit jumping, until finally you could no longer hear the sound of them hitting the lid. The lid was then removed, but not one flea tried again to jump to freedom, because they had tried and failed to do so earlier.

Do you find yourself in bad situations that seem to be "just life" but are getting worse? Are you just sitting there while these situations are destroying you? Have you tried before and failed, so you are not trying again? Could the lid have been removed, and you do not realize it because you have quit trying?

THIS VERY MINUTE

When I was a boy growing up I can remember my parents saying, "Johnny, you come hear this very minute!" I knew that meant RIGHT NOW.

There are three dimensions of time: past, present, and future. When I was ordered to come here right this minute, I knew that I was going to face the consequences of something that I had done in the past but had now come to light in the present. It could have been something that I had done just a few minutes before, but the reality of it was in this very minute. I was not punished in the past minutes when I had created the problem. I was punished in the present minute.

Memories are in the past and dreams are in the future, but experiences are only in the present. I remember wishing that what

I was experiencing would be in the past, but the pain of that act of correction was at that very minute. Memories are created by experiences. Those times are forever burned in my memory, but is it only the painful things that we remember? Could it be that there are good things that are happening to us at this very minute, and they are not even being noticed? If we do not notice the good things in the present, can they ever become a memory we can draw from? Are we so tied up in what was or what is to be that we are missing the precious experiences of this minute?

GREAT
EXPECTATIONS

As a boy, as most boys do, I fell in love with automobiles. The first car I had was a little compact that my parents gave me for my high school graduation. I was going to go to college, and it was a very practical car for me at that time. However, within a year, I had decided I needed a sports car that looked cool and would run fast. The idea of such a car absorbed my mind. I looked on every car lot I could get to, and as you can imagine, I found one. I had not established any credit, so I went to my dad and asked him to co-sign for a loan, so I could have the car of my dreams. He refused knowing the folly of such a car at that time in my life, but after going to him time and time again, he gave in against his better judgment. In the next 2 years, I had so many traffic violations that I was made to take my drivers test over, my insurance premium went through the roof, and I wrecked that car 3 times. The third time was so bad that it had to be totaled.

My expectation of the fulfillment that sports car would bring to my life was as high as it could be. But that expectation was shattered when the inevitable happened. Could it be that our greatest expectations will be blessings in our life, or could they be curses? Just because it looks like a wonderful thing today, will it turn out that way tomorrow? Is there a way to determine the outcome of our expectations?

A STRAIGHT LINE

I was taught years ago that the shortest distance between two points is a straight line. Knowing this to be the truth, I use it as we fly from place to place in our airplane. When filing my flight plan, I file direct, which is a straight line from the place of departure to the place of arrival.

In my pre-flight planning, I try to find an airport close to our concert sight. There are very helpful aviation web-sites that locate the airports close to a destination. They list them by distance from a city or town. The other day I had gone through this procedure and found the closest airport, so I filed my flight plan to that destination. Julia, our office manager, then takes the information I give her and maps out the driving directions from the airport to our concert site. When she handed me the information, the mileage from the airport to the concert site was twice as much as my aviation internet site had listed. We started to investigate the problem and found that the aviation web-site used a straight line from point to point and the highways do not always go in a straight line.

In real day to day situations, is it possible that we are always looking at the outcome as if it were a straight line? Are there curves and turns that need to be negotiated and factored in as we move from point to point? Are we disappointed when things and relationships take longer than expected? What can we do about it?

ACCEPTANCE

I was in high school in the 60's, and we had to raise the finances for most of our activities. We started in our junior year doing various things to raise the money we needed for our senior trip to Washington DC. One such fund raiser was selling magazine subscriptions. I grew up in a rural area, and everyone knew each other. Our class was very small, so I had very little competition in getting people to participate. I just went down the road and stopped at every house that did not have a student in my class, and they all bought magazine subscriptions. Some would buy two. I sold so many subscriptions that I hit the top prizes given by the magazine company as incentives for reaching certain numbers. In fact, when I got to the top and had every prize offered, I gave the rest of my sales to my best friend so he could get some prizes.

After graduating from high school and going off to college, I decided that I could make a lot of money in my spare time selling encyclopedias. It was as much a failure as the magazine subscriptions had been an overwhelming success. They were both printed material, so what was the difference? I started down the road in Columbus, Ohio and stopped at every house just as I did in our little farming community. Could it be that even selling things are built on relationships? Is it all about the sale or the cause? Do we have to build a relationship to truly be accepted?

SEASONS
of
LIFE

I have heard the expression, "in the autumn years," which, I am told, means the final years of ones life. I guess the early years of life would then be called Spring, though I can't remember hearing that one. These expressions are good for painting a picture, but the truth is that we go through many seasons in our lives and sometimes we struggle through them.

The reason for that struggle is that a new season brings about change, and we are not really comfortable with change. If we look at nature, we find that the spring brings new life, summer is a time for the crops to grow, in the autumn those crops are harvested and we are rewarded for the works of our hands, and in the winter there is a time of renewing and rest. Could it be that we only see the terrible storms in the spring, the scorching heat of summer, the death of the plants in autumn, and the bitter cold of winter? These are realities of life that are all around us. What about the seasons in our life that we cannot see, but we do experience? What is our reaction to seasons that have nothing to do with the weather? Could it be that the winter you are now going through is really a time of rest and renewal?

CARES
of
LIFE

I have been told many times that the two happiest days of a boat owners life is the day that he purchases a boat and the day that he sells it. Although this may be true most of the time, it is not true all of the time. I have seen people using their boats almost every week if the weather permits, and they really enjoy it for years. What is the difference between someone who can't wait to get rid of their boat and someone else who really enjoys theirs?

You may reason that people get a boat and then decide that they do not have enough time to use it. This can not be the primary reason because it has been proven over and over again that people make time for what they really want to do. Another possibility is that they find out that the expense to operate it is too high. This also is very unlikely because people will still, in most cases, spend whatever it takes to do what they really want to do.

In ancient Greek culture, there was a belief that every thing created had a spark of life, and that spark of life was what they were created to do. Could it be that we are all created very differently? Can we look at the things other people are enjoying and think that we would also enjoy them, when in truth, we would not? Could these things then become more trouble to us than they are worth?

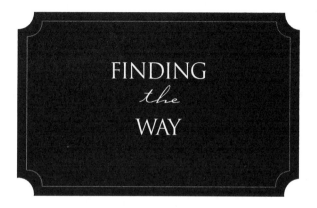

FINDING
the
WAY

We just returned from a cruise to Alaska with Dr. Charles Stanley, and while we were in Skagway, we decided to get off the ship and hike to a waterfall that was in the area. We ask directions and were told, "Just walk straight up the street a mile or so, and when you reach the old cemetery, it will be right behind it; you can not miss it." After about 20 minutes of hiking, we were running out of town, so we stopped to ask if we were headed the right way. We were once again given the same instructions as before. Another 20 minutes went by and half of our party wanted to turn back because they were convinced we were going the wrong way. About that time we looked across the street and saw some people walking the opposite direction, so we shouted to them and asked where they had been. They shouted back, "We have been to the water falls and they are a wonderful sight to behold. Keep going straight ahead, you are about half way there." Everyone was encouraged, and we hiked on for another 30 minutes never again thinking we were going the wrong way because we had talked with someone that had just been there.

Are you facing a lot of discouragement in your journey through life? Could it be that on life's road there are others that are returning from where you are going? If you could find those people, would you be able to continue to a wonderful place you might otherwise miss?

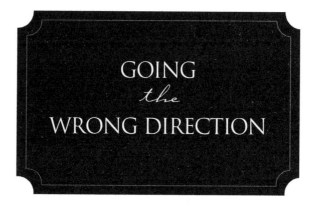

GOING
the
WRONG DIRECTION

For over 26 years, I have been traveling around the United States by car, bus, and airplane. I must say there have been times that I was going the wrong way in every one of them. (Thankfully, there was only a time or two many years ago in a plane.) You are going the wrong way and something or someone tells you, "This is not right." I remember once in Canada in the early morning I was supposed to be going east, and I noticed the shadow from the bus was on the road directly in front of me. I quickly surmised that the sun was not coming up from the west that day, so I was headed the wrong direction. I stopped, got out the map, found the way I should have been going, and turned the bus around.

We all go the wrong way in our lives at times. It happens to the best of us. Life is not about the wrong turn now and then; it is about getting back on course. In every mode of travel, there is some type of map that shows you the right way to go. When I look at the map, I do what it says, and I find my way to my destination. Did you know that life does have a map to get you where you need to go? Even if you know it exist, do you use it? Why not?

BINDING TOGETHER

Over 35 years ago, when I was being taught to roof a house, I learned that the right amount of help was needed to make the job easier. We did not have a powered lift to get the shingles on the roof or powered nailers to drive the nails. There were no dimensional shingles only three tab that had to be lined up vertically as well as horizontally. We found three men working together could accomplish more at the end of the day than all three working independently. Instead of each man carrying his own shingles up the ladder, laying the shingles in place, and then nailing them down, we had one man carry the shingles on the roof as the second man laid them in place, and the third man would do all of the nailing. Each one doing what he was best equipped to do.

In our everyday life, we have all been able to get some things done without the help of anyone, but as we all go our separate ways doing our own thing, is less getting accomplished? Is it possible that we have all been created with the same talents and gifts, or are our talents and gifts very different and designed to be part of the whole? Would it be possible to come together and get much more accomplished that each one working independently?

THE PRICE TAG

All of my life I have heard that you get what you pay for. That thought was usually voiced after buying something that did not hold up to ones expectations. So as I was growing up, my conclusion was the higher priced item would be better than the lower priced one even though they were the same thing. Well we all know that is not true in every case. Sometimes the lower priced item can be just as good or even better than the expensive one. The truth is that the quality of something is determined by the manufacturer not the price for which it is sold.

Many people do not like the way they look or the quality of life that they are experiencing. What if we could be sent back to the manufacturer for a make over? Could it be that we have judged our self worth by a false sense of our value? Have we allowed others to put a price tag on us that makes us less than we really are?

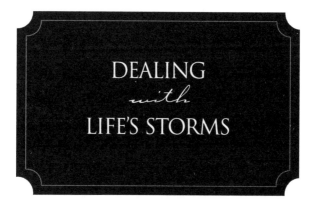

DEALING
with
LIFE'S STORMS

The other day I had a business meeting in the Charlotte, North Carolina area. We have an airplane that we travel in, so the night before the meeting, I filed a flight plan and looked over the weather. There were going to be scattered thunder storms on my way down and on the return trip home that night. Going down I was in the clouds with light to moderate rain and some light turbulence. We have on board radar and a color satellite receiver which displays green, yellow, and red read outs with red being the really bad stuff. On the way down the satellite was showing some green, so I had no problem.

Following the meeting, I returned to the airport and turned on the satellite receiver to check the weather for my flight home. There was a yellow and red path from 50 miles above Charlotte all the way to Fayette County that was 50 to 100 miles wide. I shut everything down, went to a motel, and flew home safely the next morning very thankful that I had something that would let me see the storms ahead.

We all experience life's storms from time to time. Wouldn't it be great if there was something that would show them to us so that we could avoid them? Could that be possible?

GETTING AHEAD

Many people are apprehensive about their future as our economy is experiencing a down- turn. This is an understandable reaction as we watch our 401Ks turn into a 201K. Why is it that some people come through tough times, while others cave in under the pressure?

The answer is **perspective.** People who get through tough times always look at the reality of the situation and make an effort to adapt to it, while others allow tough times to control their life. The truth is that tough times, in themselves, do not control us. If we worry and complain about our situation, we create the snow ball effect. As we worry and complain, the future seems to become darker which brings on more worry and complaining and the problem gets bigger and bigger with every cycle. Worry and complaining brings on inactivity which kills the creative ability we all are gifted with.

Most people have heard that a positive outlook is the way through tough times and that 80% of the things we worry about, never happen. That is all great, but how do we get there?

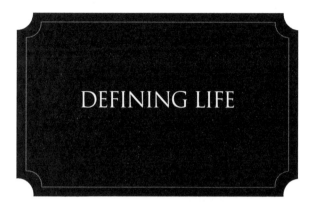

DEFINING LIFE

When I first came to this area I was a 19 year old college student driving every day from the rural Chillicothe area for summer work. Through this time, I met Glenda, who a year and a half later in 1972 became my wife. (We now have 3 children and grandchild number 8 is on the way.) I would make the drive again every Saturday and Sunday just to see Glenda. I had to spend most of my money for gasoline, but there was nothing that could have kept me from driving to Washington Court House in those days. This is where my heart was, so I had to be there.

I have heard the expression, "heart issue," all of my life. It seems that our heart can drive us to do certain things. Could it be that our heart actually defines our life? Could our life change for the better or for the worse if we have a change of heart?

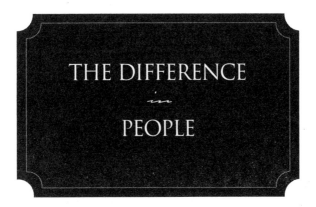

THE DIFFERENCE in PEOPLE

While traveling around the country, I have encountered all types of people. Some are financially able to wear the finest clothes made, and some are wearing soiled and worn out clothing. I find some that are timid, while others are space invaders that spit on you when they talk. There are some who wear nice smelling cologne or perfume, and some who do not wear deodorant. I meet people of every shape, size, age, and background. It is a fact that some are easier to be with than others. What is it that makes people so different? *Are all people created equal?* Is there any possibility that the space invaders and those who need deodorant are the same as the one who is in designer clothes wearing great smelling cologne? In time would I find the well dressed person more enjoyable than the space invader, or would it be the other way around?

REVERSED
PERSEPTION

Recently, I had a head light burned out in my truck. It seemed that a lot of people noticed it and let me know. While the mechanic was changing my burned out headlight, I received a voice mail on my cell phone. The message was from a lady telling me that my passengers side head light was burned out. She was mistaken because the burned out head light was on the driver's side. I had my speaker phone on when I listened to the message and the mechanic said, "that lady was ahead of you looking in her rear view mirror when she noticed the burned out head light." We had a chuckle realizing that was more than likely the case because what we see in a mirror is reversed. What is right appears left and what is left appears right. If we would have changed the burned out head light from her perception, we would have taken out the good head light and replaced it. Our effort would have been wasted, and we would not have fixed the problem. We would have still had a burned out head light on the driver's side. I wonder how many things in life are like that. Are we looking at our lives like we look at ourselves in a mirror, and what is really right appears to be left? Is it possible to tear up the good things thinking that we are repairing the bad ones?

There is an old saying that the apple does not fall far from the tree, which means that we will turn out to be very much like our parents and grandparents. There have been contradicting thoughts to this idea that state if you take a child out of their parental environment and put them in a different one, they will become a product of their new environment. Both camps seem to have numerous examples to prove their opinion. Then there are always the cases that we have all witnessed of good parents whose children turn out bad and bad parents whose children turn out good. Could it be that it is just a matter of chance, or is there something else that forms the outcome of our life?

READING
INSTRUCTIONS

I remember years ago when our children were toddlers, and my wife Glenda brought home a swing set. The swing set was in a box and needed to be assembled. I was a contractor by trade and had experience in building commercial, agricultural, and residential buildings. This swing set was no challenge for me, or so I thought. I tore the box open and started on what I thought would be a 10 minute job. The problem was that I did not take time to look at the instructions. I would put parts together and end up taking them apart because I used the wrong parts, bolts, or screws. I kept on with the task at hand by putting parts together and tearing them apart again, but I still never looked at the instructions. Keep in mind that this was over 30 years ago when swing sets had only two or three swings and a slide. Over 2 hours later, I was hooking up the chains on the cross bar.

Most of you reading this can relate because you have done the same thing. As I have gotten older, I realize that I can lay out the parts and read the instructions and it will save me a lot of time and heart ache. Do you think instructions exist on how to put our life together that would save us time and heart ache?

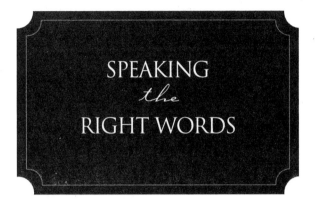

SPEAKING
the
RIGHT WORDS

 D id you ever hear the saying, "sticks and stones may break my bones, but words will never hurt me"? Our parents taught us that saying as children to help us handle the hurt we experienced when other kids would taunt and make fun of us. If we were confronted, we would try to ignore those hurtful remarks by repeating that saying over and over again. Usually we would say it out loud to the people we were having trouble with. The reality was that their teasing and making fun of us really did hurt, and we were battling the hurtful words they were speaking with words that might help us endure the pain. Another saying we were taught is, "a word once spoken can never be recalled". That saying is the absolute truth. We have learned the reality of this saying through personal experience, so how important are the words we speak? Could it be possible that we could change our situations and maybe even our life by speaking the right words? Can negative words bring on negative circumstances and positive words bring about positive experiences?

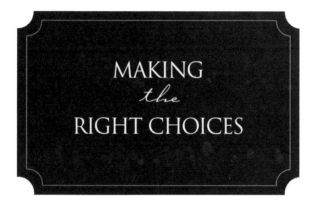

MAKING
the
RIGHT CHOICES

When I was a child, I dreamed of finding a bottle with a genie in it. If I could get my hands on such a bottle and rub it the right way, a genie would appear in a stream of smoke to grant me three wishes. I remember planning those three wishes over and over again as I was ever searching for that bottle. The first wish would always be for one million dollars. (That was a great deal of money when I was a boy.) The second wish was for a large house to live in, and the third would be that I would have the fastest hot rod in our town. If I had these things, I would be the king of the hill. As a young child these things were the limit of my expectations. As I look back on those three things, I realize that there were far bigger things I could have asked for.

Life is a series of choices. Is it possible to make choices that impact our lives as much today as they will 20 years from now?

CONCLUSION

We learn from our mistakes and also our successes. These are the simple every day experiences that all of us encounter in life. The advantage that we have over every other creature is that we have the ability to reason. Success and failure is not enough to complete our life. We must know the truth. Truth is light that is always present, and we can know it. On the other hand, there is also darkness that seeks to blind us from the truth. The good news is that light dispels darkness, and there is a powerful light that we all have available to us. There is someone to teach and lead us through every trial of life because he has experienced and conquered all of them. He has been called counselor and the prince of peace. In your quest for truth, seek him first, and everything else will be added to you!